From Shaniko *to* Pearl Harbor

by Bob Weber

The true story of
the journey of an Oregon man, and his family
To the attack of the U.S. Armed Forces
at Pearl Harbor December 7, 1941

ISBN-13: 978-09769974-0-5
ISBN-10: 0-9769974-0-1

Printed by
Gorham Printing
Rochester, Washington

This book was finished for

Bob Weber,

Who was loved so much

By so many,

But most of all, by me

With my very best wishes for your enjoyment of Bob's story. Ninette Weber

Our house on Jean Street – Territory of Hawaii

The Machinist's Mate

It was Sunday—my favorite day of the week. As the first rays of sunshine passed over the Koolau mountain range and came drifting in my bedroom window, I, Bob Weber, was up like a shot ready to enjoy another peaceful day in my cozy tropical world in the Hawaiian Islands. Unlike many teenagers, or pre-teenagers, I was never able to sleep late. There was too much to see and do, too many fish to catch. I had lived here, in Pearl City on the island of Oahu, for nearly all of my 12 years, and I had always enjoyed the peace, tranquility and pleasures that filled my life.

I hurriedly dressed and got ready for another glorious day of fishing. It didn't take long, as I rarely wore more than a pair of shorts and a tee shirt. Even shoes were optional—who needed shoes out here in the tropics?

My mother, Florence Weber, was already up fixing breakfast for me and looking forward to a trip to the Navy base to pick up my Dad, Machinist's Mate Oscar Albert Weber. He would get off duty at 8:00 A.M. and the three of us would enjoy our leisurely Sunday together.

I rushed into the kitchen and dived into my breakfast, trying to hurry, but also chatting with Mom about the new school that I had attended since September. It was my first year away from the Kapalama Grade School, where I had spent several years, and it was a bit of an adjustment. I was telling Mom about my difficulties in the music department. My new school was Robert Louis Stevenson Junior High. The faculty was very music oriented, and they had decided that each student must either be in the choir or in the band. I had definitely not inherited Dad's natural musical abilities. I had been rejected by the choir director, and now the bandleader was stuck with me. I don't think he was any happier than I was about this predicament. He assigned me an instrument similar to a French horn. It was called something like the "melaphone." Mom assured me that it would all work out and told me not to worry about it.

I finished eating, ran to brush my teeth, pausing only to let Mom know where I was going. I grabbed my fishing pole and started down the driveway. Mom came out of the house and called to me, "Hey, Bobby, why don't you come with me to pick up Daddy at the base? He would really like that."

"No," I responded, "I really need to go fishing."

She shrugged her shoulders and said, "Well, suit yourself." Mom climbed into our Model A Ford and started to back down the driveway.

For some reason—I had a change of heart just then and I called to her, "Wait a minute, I think I'll go with you."

"Oh, I'm so glad you're coming along. Daddy is always pleased when you do." I threw my fishing pole into the garage and jumped into the Model A beside her. "As it turned out it was lucky that I did change my mind, because this was not any ordinary Sunday—it was December 7, 1941 and the base

we were headed for was the submarine base at Pearl Harbor, Territory of Hawaii.

The license plate off our
Model A Ford

Hawaii was not yet a state, but was still a territory of the United States. In less than an hour we would be caught in the middle of the greatest drama of our lives. "The Day that will live in Infamy," as President Roosevelt called it, was here. It is rather amazing how fate brings you to a certain place at a certain time due to a complex convergence of circumstances. Because of a variety of unrelated happenings, Dad, Mom and I, age 12, were about to have our lives changed forever.

Bob in 1940

We drove down the street and wound our way past our neighbors and past the local farmers and their fields of vegetables and rice. It was a picturesque drive as Hawaii was a land of many cultures. Our lives were full of friends and neighbors from China, Japan, Hawaii, Portugal, and the Philippine Islands, as well as many other people and Navy friends from stateside, as we called the contingent 48 states in those days. One of my favorite sights was an elderly Chinese farmer who still plowed his land with the help of a water buffalo. He had his very own rice paddy where he, the water buffalo, and the plow, working together, made the furrows to plant the rice.

Dad's duty station was aboard the *USS Widgeon*, a submarine tender. About once a week he had the duty, which meant he stayed all night at the base. Everyone took a turn, so the facility was never left unguarded. As we neared the water at approximately 7:45 A.M., Mom maneuvered the car into our regular rendezvous spot next to the diving tower where they trained the submarine men to dive and surface safely. An enormous rope hung in the diving tower with large knots tied about 50 feet apart. The men would dive down and feel their way up to a knot, resting there a moment to protect their lungs from the dangers of coming up to the surface too fast.

It was starting to become warm and humid, so I jumped out of the car to look around and wait for Dad to arrive from the *Widgeon* and be able to leave for the weekend. I heard the noise of airplanes, looked up, and noticed an unusually large number of planes in the air. I recognized some of them as British Spitfires, a popular plane used in the British air force. I had just seen a movie, "The Battle of Britain," at the Waipahu Theatre, which had shown this plane in action. As Mom and I stood outside the car, we watched a growing number of planes flying back and forth, and they started to shoot what I was sure were fake bullets. I thought that there must be at least 50 planes in the air, but in reality, I learned later, it was 183! It wasn't long before the planes were also dropping bombs and torpedoes, some hitting their targets, some flying wild. It looked like the ships moored at Battleship Row in Pearl Harbor were being attacked also, but I felt sure that this could not be true.

Mom and I, however, had a clear front row seat to watch the most horrendous attack that the United States armed forces had ever known. The submarine base lay right across the water from Battleship Row. There were some buildings that stood between us and some of the ships, but the ships were so huge that we could see them fairly well. The most horrific thing happened next, as a bomb made a direct hit right down onto one of the battleships, the *USS Arizona*. It created a huge fireball while causing the ship to rise in the water, and then the ship broke in half, and began to rapidly sink. Everything looked so realistic to me, but I thought that it had to be just a practice drill. The word War barely existed in my vocabulary. The air started to fill with dark, black smoke and flames were shooting into the air. It became difficult for Mom and I to breathe, because the air was filled with smoke and the heavy smell of burning gunpowder. It looked like many ships had been hit, and we also heard the sound of bombs going off at Hickam Field, which lay over to our left and seaward towards the entrance to Pearl Harbor. The seaplanes on Ford Island, which lay directly ahead of us, and behind the battleships, were being strafed. I was in awe that maneuvers could look so realistic.

Suddenly Dad came running from the direction of the diving tower. "Hey Dad," I called, "how come we're having maneuvers on Sunday? I can't believe they actually blew up that battleship just for practice!"

"These aren't maneuvers," he shouted, "we're under attack."

"Oh, wow, just like 'The Battle of Britain,'" was my amazed reply. "But, Dad," I reasoned, "those are British Spitfires, why would the British attack us?"

"No, son," he said, "those are Japanese Zeroes!"

I looked again at the planes, and then I saw the rising sun emblem on the sides. The Japanese had copied the configuration of the Spitfires, so they looked a good bit alike. Because the day was warming up, some of the Japanese pilots had thrown open the canopies above their heads. As I looked up, I could see their Asian faces. It was easy to see that these pilots were not British.

For a time it was a totally one sided fight because the U.S. armed forces who were stationed on Oahu were so ill prepared. Within moments we heard loud speakers nearby blaring, "This is no drill! We are under attack! This is no drill! We are under attack!" This was repeated many times and then we heard the loud speakers announce: "We are under attack by the Empire of Japan. Man your battle stations. This is not a drill."

As I looked up into the sky, I was able to discern at least two other types of planes along with the Zeroes. About this time, a group of about a dozen U.S. B17 Flying Fortresses appeared on the scene. Unaware of the situation, they flew into the fierce battle without warning and could do nothing but merely dodge the Japanese planes

A Japanese airplane on its way to attack Pearl Harbor

and also the U.S. anti-aircraft fire. The B17s were on their way to the Philippines to bolster our Pacific forces, and they had planned to land in Hawaii to refuel before completing their journey to the South Pacific. Unfortunately, they could not have picked a worse time to arrive at Pearl Harbor. The B17s were unarmed in order to save weight for their long journey, so they were completely helpless. Luckily all the B17 pilots managed to land safely, even though not just where they had originally planned. One even ended up landing on a golf course.

Dad had seen action before, as he also was in the service during World War I, but he never had a family at his side to worry about. He glanced frantically around trying to decide what in the world to do. He was dressed in full Navy Whites, so he hastily pulled on his dungarees over the white uniform, so he wouldn't be such a distinct military target. Mom was absolutely terrified and she didn't seem to be capable of taking any action. Dad shouted to me, "Get back in the car. We've got to get your Mom out of here, and get you two to safety, then I'll hurry back and do whatever I can to help."

He climbed behind the wheel and started racing through the oil fields. It was a large field of storage oil tanks that were located behind the submarine base. The fuel stored there was basically the entire fuel supply for the U.S. defense forces in the Pacific. Dad always said how fortunate it was that the Japanese hadn't bombed those tanks of fuel to further cripple our military forces. Ordinarily we took the road beside the fields, but he chose to drive between the oil tanks because it would be faster. He turned on our car radio and we heard the frightening message: "Everyone take cover immediately."

When Dad reached the end of the field, he decided to drive up the hill to Aiea, a local town where he had a friend that he thought might help us. When we arrived, we had to pound on the door for several minutes to awaken our sleeping friend. When he finally opened the door drowsily, he was shocked to hear our news, but the evidence lay below us. We could see from his porch that the battle was in full swing. We saw the ships lying on their sides and the *USS Arizona* was barely visible from her watery grave.

We stood right about here on the submarine base.

Rescuing a survivor near The USS West Virginia.

While we stood there, I saw a couple of the Japanese planes get hit and crash. Our friend was suffering badly from a hangover that morning, so my Dad reconsidered the situation. There is something about home that spells safety to most of us, so Dad decided that we would probably be safer in our own home. We scrambled back into the car and Dad raced down the hill and headed towards Pearl City. It was about this time that a second wave of Japanese planes arrived and continued the relentless shooting and bombing. We passed other cars that had been stopped in their tracks by the Japanese bullets. When we reached the junction to Pearl City, we encountered a road-block that had been put up to keep people out of our area, since the planes were now firing and bombing in that direction. This roadblock was a good idea, because we later learned that some of the Japanese planes had crashed near our house. We also later found shrapnel and the remains of a bomb that had failed to explode inside our own house. Dad was a bit of a rugged individualist but never stupid so he obeyed the

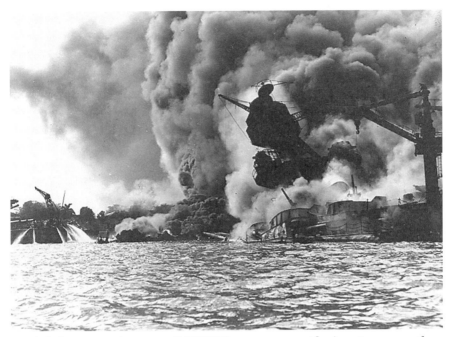

At left, men on the stern of USS Tennessee *are playing streams on the water to force burning oil of* the USS Arizona *away from their ship.*

roadblock, turned around, and drove up to the Waipahu Sugar Plantation where his friend, Jack Vorfeld, was the manager.

As we drove up the hill towards Waipahu, we looked back at that dreadful scene and wondered how we had gotten away safely. There were other cars that had been strafed and the occupants killed. I wondered why we hadn't met the same fate. Years later my Mother still stressed over how dreadful it would have been if I had chosen to go fishing that Sunday morning and had not been safe with her and Dad.

At the sugar plantation, the Vorfeld's were gathered inside their house and were listening to the ear-splitting sounds of bombs and machine guns, and we were able to verify that the worst was, in fact, happening. Dad unloaded us from the car and took Mom aside.

"I don't know where things will go from here, but if it gets too bad," he said, "keep this pistol with you for protection, or if you really need a way out, you'll have a way to escape from the horrors that we

The USS Utah

may all face. I love you, and I hope that, God willing, I'll see you and Bobby again soon. I must get back down to the base and try to help my shipmates any way that I can." So off he went, driving down the hill and back to Pearl Harbor as fast as the Model A could go.

We stood there, in shock, and watched Dad go racing down the hill to do his duty and help as best he could. Mom held me close until he was out of sight, and then steered me up to the Vorfeld's house.

We spent an uneventful afternoon and evening, and I got interested in playing with the Vorfeld's young children, helping to entertain them, while the adults huddled around the kitchen table and tried to decipher the awful sounds that rose from the base at Pearl Harbor.

Eventually Mom called me to her, and said, "It's time to get to bed. We need to get a good night's rest so we'll be ready to welcome Daddy home in the morning. I'm sure he'll have a rough night."

I obediently bedded down with the Vorfeld kids in some borrowed pajamas, and with the carefree mind of a 12 year old, I soon fell fast asleep confident that all would be well in the morning.

The Runaway/
The Cowboy

My mother, however, older and wiser, spent a restless night. She would drift off to sleep periodically, only to be awakened by the sound of anti-aircraft fire. The U.S. military was shooting occasionally throughout the night hoping to avoid another attack by the Japanese aircraft.

As Mom lay there, her mind drifted back over the years and she recalled the wonderful life that she and Dad had enjoyed these past 13 years.

Florence Schneider met Oscar Weber in the early 1900s when she was still a young girl. They lived in Portland, Oregon, where their mothers were great friends and the two families shared many activities together. They had even gone camping together and shared a tent. Florence remembered Oscar as the renegade amongst the two families. She was nearly a year older than he was, and she thought he was just a bit of a wild kid. The families had five children between them at the time, but Oscar was the one who never seemed to want to conform.

When he was 15, in the year 1908, he decided that he was all grown up. He wanted to get away and start his adult life, so he got up early one morning while the rest of the family slept, and sneaked out of the house. He headed east towards Troutdale, a suburb of Portland. He walked all day long, and finally reached his destination just as the last rays of daylight were ebbing away. Today that trek from Portland to Troutdale would take less than a half hour by car, but the early 1900s were different times. There were no freeways, and there were very few cars on the roads. Oscar encountered another run-away and together the two boys decided to push on to Corbett, Oregon, a town a bit further east yet. When they reached this small community, they were pretty well tired out, and they spent the night in a bunkhouse. Oscar reported later to his Mom," I ditched the other kid the next morning."

On that day, Oscar's second day away from home, he hiked to the next town. It was the town of Bridal Veil. He found a train that was making a brief stop, and had a freight car with an open door. Oscar climbed hastily aboard. The car was full of railroad ties, and was headed for the town of Hood River in the Columbia River Gorge. Oscar spent his second night away from home sleeping in a boxcar in Hood River. He then boarded a passenger train and headed for another little town named Shaniko, located in Central Oregon. Shaniko was a small town that Oscar chose as his final destination. The town still exists, but there isn't much there except the restored Shaniko hotel, a few old buildings and a great deal of peace and quiet. That night, as Oscar eventually wrote to his Mom, "I slept like a prince—in a stable, with a borrowed bearskin as a blanket." The 18-year-old kid who loaned it to him reported that he had shot the bear himself. I think Oscar liked this fact. It seemed to make the bearskin more special to him.

The proprietor gave Oscar some writing paper and a stamp so he could let his family know how he was doing. He tried to pay the man for the paper and stamp, but the man told Oscar, "A fellow is darn low when he takes 2 cents from a kid."

Shaniko, Oregon in 1908

While on the passenger train to Shaniko, Oscar met a man and his wife who owned a cattle ranch and they asked Oscar to come work for them. As he reported, "They thought I was an honesty boy." The life they described sounded like the very life he was looking for. Oscar had a deep and permanent love of horses that stayed with him all the days of his life. On this night, the third one after leaving home, he stayed once again in a stable. That night he found time to write to his Mama. He closed his letter with the admonition, "Don't write 'till I get there, so you'll know the address." When they were at last home at the ranch, the couple gave Oscar a bed in the bunkhouse, and he fell fast asleep dreaming of the wonderful job he had found.

His mother was pretty hysterical by the time she got his letter, but all she could do was wait for another letter, and find out where he had ended up. So the rebel boy got to stay in Eastern Oregon and pursue his dream. The ranch was located in the Oregon High Desert country in Crook County.

Florence remembered how shocked she was when she learned that Oscar had run away from home while he was still only 15 years old.

OFFICE OF
Cornett Stage & Stable Co.

Shaniko, Oregon, April 4   190_8_

Dear mama

    I thought I would drop a few lines to you to let you know where I am at. The first day I made Troutdale and that evening I met a kid about 21 years old ~~we~~ ~~walk up to~~ walkitt and got off with ~~out~~ ~~paying~~ and slept in a bunk house then I skipped him.

~~one of the~~ The second day I rode on a car of ties from Bridal veil up to Hood river there I slept in a box car and then took the passenger for Shaniko. Last night I slept like a prince in the stage stable the prop is a good fellow, He gave me this writing paper and stamps and when I wanted to give him some money He said, "A fellow is dam low when he takes 2 cent. I met a lady on the train and she wants me to go with her so I am her husband to here in ~~him~~ getting provision he has got four big horse

we are going to summer lake The lady said I shouldn't stay with her because I look like an honesty boy

    You ought to see the cow puncher here in town, And when the stage pull out the horse buck like the dickim

    Last night I was kind of cold and a stage driver pull in he was about 18 years old

    He gave me 2 bag ~~b~~ blanket and a bear robe what he shot him self

    This is like a frontier town about every saloon there is a dozen faroe stand there

    Every body said that I got a good place now We expect to make ~~prineville~~ to day

        Your son

            Oscar Nelson

P.S. Don't write till I get there so you know

Oscar's first letter home

18

She always followed the straight and narrow path, doing as she was told, and she couldn't imagine anyone even younger than she was, forging out alone.

When Oscar awakened the next morning in the bunkhouse, he decided that he had made a wonderful choice. It was an outstanding ranch for the times, and Oscar was well received by the other ranch hands. He was asked to sing to entertain the older men around the campfires in the evening, and they seemed to enjoy his songs and accepted him as a promising new cowboy. He learned to ride like a pro and rope cattle, pitch hay, and break colts to the saddle. The men also taught him to hunt and fish, and hang around with the best of them.

The drawbacks to life in Eastern Oregon were several: fruit was scarce, communications were very slow, and the nearest neighbor was 49 miles away. The newspaper from Portland took two weeks to arrive in Crook County. Oscar reported that some Indians brought the paper to the ranch. He admired the Indians that he met in Eastern Oregon and he read a lot of stories about them and their lives. He remained a big fan of Chief Joseph, and learned everything that he could about this Indian hero. Eventually Oscar's father traveled from Portland and tracked him down, but Oscar convinced him that he was doing fine. His parents decided to let him stay at the ranch as long as he kept them informed.

A year after leaving home, Oscar decided that he wanted to join the Army Cavalry where he could serve his country and be with his beloved horses. His parents were too far away to sign for him, and besides he was only 16, so he talked one of the local women into signing for him to join, attesting to the fact that he was 17 years old. The Cavalry, however, was not hiring at the time, so Oscar continued his life as a ranch hand.

He enjoyed his western style life, became totally at home in the saddle, and pretty much was able to outride most of the men around. He also took a stint as a stagecoach driver, where he really enjoyed frightening the city slickers who had the dubious luck to board his rig. He wrote home, telling of an incident where he drove the stage down a slippery, steep, icy road. His passenger was terrified as Oscar whipped the horses to make them go as fast as they could. As he reported to his Mom, "Well, I couldn't go no slower. I had to make them go as fast as they could. The stage was rolling at an unbelievable speed. If the horses didn't race, the stagecoach would run over them and kill them." Oscar apparently moved around Eastern Oregon, and part of Idaho quite a bit. He had many jobs in many towns. He learned to harrow, plant seeds, pitch hay, run a thresher, and help out with just about anything a farm hand/cowboy could do. Oscar continued this western style life until September of 1914.

The Webers & The Schneiders – Florence 3rd from right, Oscar far right
1907

The Recruit

At this time, while on a visit home to Portland, Oscar Weber decided to ask Florence Schneider to marry him. She was working as a milliner making hats for ladies at a downtown department store, Meier & Frank. She refused his offer, knowing she wouldn't fit into his rough, western lifestyle. The war was raging in Europe, and life seemed very uncertain. Oscar thought things over, and he decided to join the Navy. This was a momentous decision for him, because as it turned out, Oscar stayed on active and inactive duty with the Navy for the rest of his life. He served over forty years and in 1954 received a letter of commendation from the Secretary of the Navy, Charles S. Thomas, who congratulated him on forty years service for the Department of Defense.

Joining the Navy made a bit of an unusual life for Oscar. He was a deep-water sailor, working aboard ships and submarines, including the *USS Hartford*, the *USS Parrott*, and the *USS Beaver*. But Oscar also remained a dry land cowboy whenever he got the chance.

Oscar never went to school beyond the 8th grade but he became reasonably well educated by reading as much as he could. He also could remember what he read to an unusually high degree. He read most everything that he could get his hands on, including the Holy Bible. Once, while on a tour of submarine duty, the Captain noticed Oscar reading during his off duty time. The Captain said to him, "Weber, you must be the best read man in the United States Navy." Oscar was quite proud of these words coming from the Captain of the ship.

Emil Weber and his son,
Seaman Oscar Weber

In 1917 America joined the World War I effort after the Germans sunk several American ships in the Atlantic Ocean. It became apparent to President Woodrow Wilson that America could no longer remain neutral and he could not convince the other peace loving countries that peace was a possibility. So, after three years in the Navy, Oscar found himself in the middle of World War I. He served as a machinist's mate and was stationed in Turkey following the war. While in Turkey, true to his outgoing nature and his enthusiasm for life, Oscar raised cane now and again. It is reported that he even rode either a horse or a camel into a bar at one time! He was such a rascal that he was fond of bragging that he was in the Navy for over 40 years, and never received a good conduct medal. His war records, however, show that this was not true. He just thought it made a good story. In fact he received more than one good conduct award.

IN ALL PARTS
OF THE
WORLD
THE RECOGNIZED
REPRESENTATIVES
OF
LIBERTY,
JUSTICE
AND EQUALITY

Oscar's photo in the Portland Telegram *newspaper*

Another antic that Dad told me about was the time that he and several shipmates decided to smuggle some Turkish liquor onto their ship in the Turkish harbor. The sailors had all been in town partying and they decided to bring back some of the beverages. They were checked for this contraband as they were piped back aboard the ship. There was, at that time, a custom in Turkey, where if your house caught fire, you would call for help saying something that sounded like "Yung an var!" Local unofficial firefighters would come running and bid for the job of dousing the

Oscar with first wife, Evdoxia

flames. Until you agreed on a price, your house continued to burn. Of course this caused great confusion. So while some of the sailors stayed on the dock with the booze, the rest of them passed inspection and boarded the ship. They ran around to the stern of the boat and shouted "Yung an var!!" The Captain of the large Turkish cruiser parked next to them thought the U.S. ship was on fire, so he ordered his men to spray the ship down good with their fire hoses. During the confusion, it was easy for the shipmates with the liquor to race on board, and stash their party supplies.

Oscar must have slipped around the Mediterranean a bit doing some sight seeing, and eventually he met and married a pretty little Greek girl. He was transferred back to the states, but his marriage did not last long, as his young wife contracted tuberculosis and died within a short time. He devoted his energy for the next few years to working hard for the U.S. Navy. He was stationed at Mare Island in California, but took tours of duty with the submarines in various ports, including the Philippine Islands. Somehow Oscar could never forget that darling girl, Florence, who had had a piece of his heart for most of his life. However, he came close to losing any chance of having her for his own when he got quite drunk one night, and wrote her a letter admitting that he had been less than a saint. In the letter he also hinted that she probably wasn't always decent either. Florence answered with a letter that, as Oscar wrote to his sister Edna, "Hit me between the Barbette and the engine room." Hastily, he wrote again, apologized to her and prayed that he was back in "smooth waters." .

The newly wed Webers

The Husband

Along about 1928, while home on leave in Portland, Oscar again approached my Mom to be, Florence, and asked her to marry him. At this time she felt that he had matured enough to be a good husband, so they were married in San Francisco and started their life together there. About a year later, they were expecting a baby while living on Goat Island, as they called it, in San Francisco Bay. I believe this was the island that was later enlarged and became the site for the 1939 San Francisco World's Fair.

As the time for the baby to arrive drew near, Florence became anxious. It was necessary to go by boat to reach the hospital, because none of the San Francisco bridges had yet been built.

One night in July of 1929 Oscar left the island to help one of his shipmates transport his pregnant wife to the hospital to deliver their child. Just as they returned home to Goat Island, Florence said, "We'd better go back to the hospital. I think our baby is coming today also." So the men jumped back into the Navy boat, helped Florence aboard, and took off for Letterman General Hospital in the Presidio in San Francisco. About halfway there, the engine on the boat died, and Florence spent an anxious 20 minutes while her heroes tried to get the

Marty Donlan – The Navy Boxing Champ

engine restarted, and while the tide tried to send them out to sea. Eventually the fellows got the engine started and they reached the hospital in time for an Army doctor, Major Villars, to be the first person to see me, Robert Donlan Weber, as I entered this world at 7:00 P.M. on Sunday, July 14, 1929.

The way I received my name was a testimony to the fact that Dad was an honest man. He always said to me, "Keep your word! If you make a promise, you are honor bound to fulfill that promise." Earlier, in 1925, while on a tour of duty in the Philippine Islands, he had made such a promise. At that time his ship had a group of amateur boxers aboard. They liked to box with the men from the other ships, other branches of the service, and even men from other countries. Oscar was the head trainer for his group of Navy boxers. One night, possibly while out partying, he made a deal with one of the Philippine personnel that he would bring his best fighter to compete against the best Philippine fighter available. The best fighter in Oscar's group was his good friend, Marty Donlan. The deal was agreed upon, and Oscar just needed to get Marty ready to fight the next night.

He found Marty shooting pool and relaxing at the NCO (non-commissioned officer's) club. "Hey, Donlan," he shouted, "I've got a great deal going. Tomorrow you're going to fight the best fighter on the Philippine ship."

"Nothing doing," Marty retorted, "I just don't feel like fighting tomorrow."

"Oh, Hell!" Oscar said, "You've got to do this. I promised."

"Naw," Marty said, "I just don't feel like it. Go get someone else."

Oscar left the room dejected, and tried to figure out who else could do as well as Marty Donlan. He didn't want the U.S. Navy to look like no shows or quitters. When Donlan came back to their quarters, Oscar again pleaded with him to do it. "I don't care if you win, lose, or draw, just do it. I'll tell you what, if you will do this for me, I will name my first born son after you."

This offer caught Donlan off guard. "Damn it all, Oscar," he said, "if you feel that strongly about it, I'll do it."

Most of the fighters led with their right hands, and apparently Donlan led with his left. The other fighter came out swinging with his right hand, and ready to dodge a right hand counter attack. Donlan had a powerful left hook, and he let it go full bore. His opponent staggered and fell to the ground. It was the U.S. Navy by a knockout. Needless to say, the whole ship was delighted. They had probably wagered on the fight, and were most happy to have Donlan win. Four years passed before Oscar was able to make good on his promise. When I made my appearance in the delivery room at

Little Bob Weber

Letterman General Hospital on July 14, 1929, sure enough, I was named Robert DONLAN Weber.

So here I was and my mother and father never had another child. Mom always said that she got what she wanted the first time, so there was no need to have another. I always felt a strong love from both of my parents. I always knew that I was just what they wanted. That is a wonderful feeling for a child to have while he is growing up.

The Webers

The Hawaiian

Six months later when the Navy decided to send Dad to Hawaii, my parents were very pleased. Who wouldn't want to live in the warm tropics of the Hawaiian Islands? Years later Dad confided in me one of the reasons that he liked Hawaii so well. "Gosh, Bob," he said, "one of the best things about living here is that you're 3000 miles from your nearest relative."

I grew up in a delightful place, enjoying the sunshine, and learning all the ways to enjoy the warm waters of the Pacific Ocean and the lovely land. Life was a bit more interesting than it would be in many places. When I was only one year old, Dad decided to leave the Service, but to continue to work for the Navy as a civilian employee. He also stayed in the Navy Reserve, keeping a close tie to the life we had all enjoyed.

There were lots of advantages to

Hilo Hattie

31

Oscar, the Hawaiian cowboy

staying in the reserve. We were able to receive many benefits, such as shopping at the Navy Exchange and attending the Christmas celebrations at the base. He became a mechanic at the Navy base as a civilian employee, made close friends of the many local cowboys, and met lots of other colorful people. Surprisingly enough, there were

The Webers with two friends

many horses in the islands. And there is even at least one huge horse ranch on the Big Island, so Dad was in his glory. He now had Florence, the wife that he had always wanted, a son called Robert Donlan Weber, a job that he liked, tropical weather that couldn't be beat, and a treasured hobby with his horse and his cowboy friends. The cowboys, like the rest of the population in the Hawaiian Islands, were a mix of races and cultures including Polynesian, Portuguese, Japanese and Chinese. The cowboys were called paniola, a contraction of a Spanish word. There were at one time 328 ranches in the Hawaiian Islands. Of this number, only about ten ranches were on Oahu, but that was plenty for a part time cowboy like Oscar. Cowboys frequently have close friendships, and Dad always met and bonded with horsemen wherever he lived.

Growing up in Hawaii provided me with several unique activities. Some things were okay to do, and some that we young boys probably shouldn't have done. One of our less acceptable tricks as young lads was placing rocks on the railroad tracks to jiggle the pineapple trains

Resting on a tree trunk

that would come down from the plantation loaded to the top with juicy, ripe pineapples. My friends and I would wait for the train to hit the rocks, jiggle their load of pineapples, and watch for some to fall off. Then we would rescue them, and spend a happy afternoon munching on our contraband fruit. Another one of our favorite tricks was to sneak into Buddhist wedding receptions and try to look like guests in order to sample their food. They always had the best food in town. Their funeral processions were an attraction for us, too. The bereaved family would wrap coins in colorful papers with ribbons tied around them, and toss them out of the family car as it traveled to the cemetery.

One negative side to living in Hawaii was the many insects, because of the tropical weather. When we were lucky enough to move into a brand new house, my mother was excited as she assumed there would be no bugs, at least for a time. Much to her dismay, some cockroaches moved in before we did. She just had to put up with the uninvited insects, unfortunately, although she had never had similar experiences growing up in Portland, Oregon. One group of little pests that I enjoyed was the wee little lizards. I called them "little woos" when I was small. They were very prevalent, but not much of a problem as far as I know. There was one group of tiny insects that we called "no see-ums." They were very tiny, but they always appeared if we were careless and left food out. This taught us to be careful with covering and storing food.

When it was time to attend school, I started at the August Ahrens School in Waipahu. School was such a mixture of cultures and languages. I was quite blond as a boy, and I was one of only a few fair-haired kids. The rest of the schoolchildren were Chinese, Japanese, Hawaiian, Filipino, and Portuguese. Although the children all spoke the languages from these countries, there was one more language used by many of the local people, called Pigeon English. Many of the students spoke their own style of English, peppered with a bit of many dialects. This made it rather hard for a newcomer to understand and communicate. On the first day of school the class was divided in half. The teacher said, "If you speak English go to this side of the room. If you do not speak English go over there." This had to be

Bob's first school

repeated in several languages before the students all understood the directions. The quality of education suffered some from the time spent trying to get everyone to know what was going on.

There was one teacher in the district named Clara Haili Inter. She became a world famous entertainer during World War II. She was nicknamed Hilo Hattie because she sang the song of this name. She did the Hula, played her ukulele, and sang Hawaiian songs to the delight of her many fans. Later some dress shops named after Hilo Hattie helped keep her name alive in Hawaiian folklore.

Dad, Mom and I absorbed a lot of Hawaiian culture, and used quite a bit of the Hawaiian language as our own. Then, like now, everyone used the greeting *Aloha* to mean hello, goodbye, and also as a term of affection. We learned about the *menehunes*, the Hawaiian equivalent of the Irish leprechaun. Dad often referred to something he didn't quite believe as *hoomalimali*. We all knew that *kane* was a man, *wahine* was a woman, and a child was called a *keiki*. There were a lot of places around the Navy base marked *KAPU!* This meant "KEEP OUT" in no uncertain terms. Another word that my Dad used a lot was *malia, malia,* to mean "slow and easy. I'm not sure if this is a Hawaiian word or not. When we were in downtown Honolulu we never heard people say, "north, south, east or west." They would say, Pearl Harbor, Diamond Head, *Mauna* (toward the mountains), or *Makai* (toward the sea). In later years my Dad even owned a horse that he named Ehu. I later learned that in the Hawaiian language *ehu* means a sandy-colored reddish hue. This described Ehu for he was a chestnut colored animal.

While still in grade school, I started coming home with wondrous tales of my new hero, the Navy school bus driver. Dad was impressed as I kept repeating the phrase that, "The bus driver says...." The bus driver seemed to know just about everything, at least according to me. Dad got so curious that eventually he investigated and came home pretty disgusted. Mom met him at the door, and he blurted out, "That bus driver, hell, he's nothing but a 17 year-old red headed kid."

Actually the bus driver didn't stay my hero for long. Dad was my real hero. We were pretty good friends, and we hung out together a lot. I tried, but I just didn't have the love of horses that he did. On the other hand, he didn't love fishing the way I did. However, I rode with him, and he fished with me. This kept us both happy.

We spent quite a lot of time in the water. The warm, ocean waters were right there, and I even learned to ride a surfboard at a very young age. There were also rain forests up in the hills to visit. One site that our family loved to visit was a waterfall that was so private that eventually we took to skinny-dipping there. I think I really enjoyed the slightly sinful feeling that it gave me, although it was totally private, and we were never intruded upon.

Match books that were part of Bob's collection

When I was still fairly young, a friend and I embarked on our first money-making experience. We bought some shoe shining equipment and we would go down to the dock where the sailors landed to come ashore. They were frequently on their way to the Monkey Bar at the Pearl City Tavern when they weren't on duty. We made some good pocket money by shining their black shoes up pretty well. The sailors paid us rather generously, plus there was the added bonus of free matchbooks that they often gave to us. The matchbooks had the names and pictures of their ships imprinted on them. We tried hard to get one from each ship that came into port. I had souvenirs like this from nearly every ship that was attacked on December 7th. I was never sure which of our customers survived the vicious attack, because living up at the sugar plantation put us too far away to continue with our shoe-shine business. The men weren't as worried about how their shoes looked after that dreadful December 7th either.

One of the places that Dad liked to take me was to the home of the German counsel. I believe his last name was Koontz. He had a son about my age, and the boy had the most intriguing European toys. I was particularly fascinated with his collection of German tin soldiers. They had the ability to raise their arms in the Heil Hitler signal, just like the real soldiers did. The word *heil* is the German word for hail. This salute was used by the German soldiers and always looked a bit silly to me. Some of the tin soldiers also marched, raising their legs high in a goose step, just like the real German soldiers did. There were also little German flags with swastikas on them, just like the large German flags that we all grew to hate after America entered the war.

After the attack on Pearl Harbor, Dad was called up before the review board because they wanted to know about his relationship with this German counsel. The license plate on Dad's car had been spotted when we visited their home. The board of inquiry asked if he had, indeed, been there.

"Yes, sir," he answered in the affirmative.

"Well, didn't you know he was a spy?" was the curt question.

"I kind of thought he must be," Oscar answered.

"What made you think so?"

"I figured no one got out of Germany with any wealth at that time, and he seemed to have plenty."

"Why didn't you report it to us?" the officer asked.

"I had no proof, and I knew you knew he was here. Would you have believed me if I had said, 'I think he's a spy?'"

"No, I guess not," was the man's slow response.

"That's why I didn't report it to you. I really had nothing to report."

"Why did you visit so often?" was the last question.

"Gosh," answered Oscar, "he had the best German beer and the best German sausage in the islands."

One wonderful lesson that I learned from Dad is that there are good people in every walk of life. You may not like everything that some of them do, but you can still have respect for, and like good people, whoever they may be.

Along with the German Counsel, Dad had many friends, both in low and high places. He had a good friend named Willy Ho. Willy and his family were a Chinese family who owned a gas station and a grocery store where we did a lot of shopping. Dad also had a friend who was the matron at the women's prison. She was a charming Hawaiian woman. We learned a great deal about the different cultures from these friends. The Hawaiian lady once told me something about her grandchild. I asked, "How many children did you have?"

She answered, "Oh, I never had any children."

"How did you get the grandchild?" I asked.

"Years ago we found a baby girl on our doorstep. No one claimed her, so we were able to keep her. Then my sister's husband passed away, and she gave me her daughter, so the child would have two parents. Then, later, we received a young boy, the son of my husband's brother. He was their 13th child, so they decided to let us have a son to

The China Clipper *on her first arrival in Hawaii*

raise. In fact, the house we live in was given to us by his real father, so he would have a place like his other siblings did."

I got the impression that this was not unusual in the Hawaiian community, to do what was best for a child.

Another interesting friend of Dad's owned one of the hotels in downtown Honolulu. It was on Hotel Street, which was the heart of the red light district. Strangely enough the YMCA was right next door. Dad used to take me to this hotel while he had a beer with the owner. The ladies who worked there were of many nationalities, and they made quite a fuss over me, this young blond haired boy. They told me they liked my blond hair and "big brown eyes." At my age I had no idea what went on there in the red light district. As far as I know, we never went there when the place was open for business.

I think that Dad's friendliness to such an assortment of people helped me to later, as an adult, become a successful retail furniture and appliance salesman. I tried never to judge our customers by outward appearances. A poor but honest family needed a refrigerator just as badly as the rich families. I tried to treat all people with respect just as he did his myriad friends from most any background.

One day in 1937 stands out in my memory. It was the day that the China Clipper aircraft landed near our house. The whole town of Pearl City, and probably much of Honolulu turned out to welcome the first plane to start a regular mail and passenger service between the mainland and Hawaii. The China Clipper continued on to Guam, Midway, and the Philippine Islands. I remember there were about 3000 people who came down to the landing to see this first plane bring the mail and the first passengers on a regularly scheduled flight to the islands. This was the jumbo airplane of its time. It was a 4-engine flying boat with a nose similar to the modern 747 that was built many years later. Mom took my picture standing next to the giant plane. We thought we would never again see such a mighty ship. The ship was a Martin M-130, but before long it was nearly always called the China Clipper in honor of the clipper ships that had sailed the seven seas of the world. These planes were owned by Pan American Airlines. Martin had built a fleet of three of these clipper ships, but all three of them were eventually involved in fatal crashes. The last China Clipper to crash was destroyed in a botched landing off Trinidad in 1945, after she had flown over three million miles. I believe it was the same plane whose arrival in Hawaii we had watched with such awe and respect.

After three years in August Aherns school, it was time for me to move on to Kapalama Intermediate School. I remember it was quite a trip to get to school. Mom would take me to the dock and put me on a motor sailor, a small boat that ferried us over to Ford Island. We would disembark the motor sailor and then climb aboard a ferry to continue on to the far shore. A bus picked us up at that point and drove the rest of the way to school. Mom had warned me not to run on the boat, so I skipped as fast as I could to get around on the boats. I'm not sure she would have approved of this, but I am sure she never thought to tell me, "Don't skip."

We didn't visit the regular tourist locations very often, but when we entertained visitors from the states, the U.S. mainland, we showed them around. My favorite visitor was my Aunt Alyce, mother's youngest sister. She was a very pretty, young, unmarried schoolteacher at the time and she came to see what the Hawaiian Islands were like. She loved it there and we had a good time showing her around. I remember there were only two luxury hotels on Waikiki beach at that time, the Royal Hawaiian and, I believe, the Moana. It is hard to imagine now but Honolulu was still a lazy, little community without a lot of traffic, and not a huge number of tourists. In my younger years, people had to come by ship, so it was a time consuming trip. When Aunt Alyce arrived, we decorated her with colorful leis and showed her some of the Hawaiian sights. I loved to show people the Bishop Museum because it contained so much of Hawaii's early history. It was fascinating to live in a place that had previously been governed by a king and queen. The tales of King Kamehameha were familiar to me as a child and the parades always featured lots of old Hawaiian folklore.

One day in 1937 Dad came home from work quite outraged. "They've sunk the *Panay*," he reported. "That does it, I'm going back in the service." It was the Japanese who had sunk the *USS Panay*, a shallow draft river gunboat built to protect American interests along the Yangtze River during the Chinese civil war. The boat was in the process of evacuating Americans from Nanking prior to the Japanese occupation of the city. The dive-bombers and fighters from Japan unexpectedly attacked the *USS Panay* and the gunboat sank rapidly. The Japanese government immediately apologized for the action, however, so my Dad decided not to join at that point.

However, on November 11, 1940 when he was recalled to active duty, he went willingly and headed down to the base to get his assignment. The officer welcomed him back, and Oscar voiced his wish to get assigned to a submarine once again. "Hey grandpa," the young man said, "you're too old to be on a sub. That's not appropriate duty for someone your age."

Oscar must have been about 40 at the time. He came home in quite an angry mood. "That young whipper-snapper, I could teach him a thing or two about subs." But the ruling stood firm, and Dad accepted an assignment aboard the *USS Widgeon*, a submarine tender.

His years on board a sub helped Dad understand how the *Widgeon* could help a submarine in distress. One maneuver they took part in was to practice rescuing a lost submarine. Of all the men involved, Dad had the best record for finding a sub that was hiding. Finally his commanding officer demanded to know how he did it. "It's easy," Oscar said. "Just wait until 8:00 a.m. when the shifts change. The men who worked all night will go to bed, after first stopping in the head (Navy word for bathroom). Just watch the sea, and you'll see the toilet paper swirl up through the water."

It kind of shows you that Oscar was always thinking. He just seemed to have a great supply of common sense. As the saying goes, "Common sense to an uncommon degree is what the world calls wisdom." I learned that quote later from one of my high school teachers.

Of course Dad's antics occasionally got him into trouble. Once, while he was out rescuing dummy torpedoes dropped on practice runs by some of our airplanes, one of the two man planes got in trouble. It was apparent that the airplane was going to crash, and it was necessary to let the navigator parachute out first. The pilot panicked and threw his canopy back, trapping the navigator in his seat. The pilot bailed out and parachuted to safety, but Oscar watched the plane crash and he knew the navigator had died. The destroyer that had been monitoring the operation signaled Oscar to go pick up the pilot. Oscar ignored the signal, and the destroyer crew had to pick up the pilot themselves. So, of course, Dad had to face a Navy Inquiry group and the Shore Patrol when he got back to shore. They probably threw him in the brig to wait for the Captain's hearing to determine what to do with the man who had disobeyed orders. When Oscar faced the Captain at the hearing, he was asked, "Didn't you see the signal to pick up the pilot?"

"Yes," he answered, "But I figured the son of a bitch could swim to shore. He had just killed his shipmate, and that's not the way the Navy has ever behaved in my lifetime. You just don't save yourself at the expense of your shipmate."

Oscar was acquitted of the charge of disobeying orders. Dad later said that he was lucky, as the Captain who tried him was an old time captain who believed in the same code of honor that Oscar followed.

Life at home in Pearl City didn't change much after Dad was recalled to active duty because we had always had close ties to Navy life. The fact that Dad was, once again, on active duty didn't seem too significant to me. And so we continued with our peaceful existence until that fateful day, Sunday, December 7th, 1941.

Aunt Alyce arrives to visit

The Hero

When I awoke in the Vorfeld's house up at the sugar plantation on Monday December 8, 1941, Mother was sitting at the kitchen table. She was talking with the Vorfelds and trying to figure out what was going on. We assumed that Dad would arrive soon from down below at Pearl Harbor, and fill us in with news. "Have some cereal, Bubby," Mom said.

"I think I'll wait and eat with Dad," I answered. I decided to wander outside and see if anything interesting was going on. I walked down by the sugar refinery, but I didn't see anyone around. Most of the workers at the plantation were Japanese, and I think they probably didn't know if they would be welcome or not.

As far as we now know, they were all pro-American, and they had no prior knowledge of this horrendous attack. Jack Vorfeld came to the refinery and we shared our thoughts about what could be happening to my Dad. He offered me a stalk of sugar cane to chew on. I always enjoyed this, but soon I felt like I had better go get some real breakfast. I went back to the house, but our Ford was still not in the

The menu from Christmas dinner – 1941

driveway. "Come on, Bobby," Mom said, "Daddy must be held up. You eat now, and he'll eat when he gets here."

So the day droned on and on. Once we heard a car approaching the house and we thought that it must be Dad. Instead it was a man from the Salvation Army. He gave each of us a new toothbrush, one of the many things we were missing. I have since then had a soft spot in my heart for the Salvation Army, so they always received donations from me. I guess my donations were a thank you for that welcome toothbrush.

It is hard for the hours to pass when you are waiting for something important to happen especially when you're only 12 years old. As it was, we waited all day, with no sign of Dad, and no message from him. We went to bed on Monday night still uncertain of where he was and whether or not he was safe. When we got up on Tuesday, I saw that the driveway was still empty, and I started to get a knot in my stomach. I wondered what could have happened to Dad. We had heard rumors of the enormous number of casualties, so it was hard not to fear the worst. The day dragged slowly by, and once again, we went to bed with no news from Dad. On the third day Mom and I were out in the back yard when we heard a car drive up front. We ran across the yard and as we rounded the corner of the house, we caught sight of a very tired and haggard looking seaman, my Dad. Mom and I both cried and fell into his arms for a grateful reunion. "Dad," I asked, "did anyone we know get killed?" The bad news was that quite a few men had died who were personal friends of his.

He said, "You remember those two pilots, the Morman boys that we liked so well. They went out as a Dawn Patrol. They never came back, so I guess they were shot down by some of those planes that we saw." Dad explained that he had spent all three days helping to rescue the survivors of the attack, and also helping to retrieve the bodies of the less fortunate souls.

Dad always had a rather large vocabulary of swear words and, believe me, we heard lots of them that day! I suppose many of his swear words came from his days as a young cowboy, and probably many more from the life of a sailor. He tried not to swear too much in front of me, at my young age, but it was so much a part of his vocabulary that he just couldn't seem to talk without peppering his speech with a few choice words. Once, a neighbor girl asked her Mom, "Mother, is the Jesus Christ that Mr. Weber talks about the same one that we talk about in Sunday School?"

Well, Oscar couldn't quit cursing at the fate that had trapped so many men inside the *USS Arizona* at Pearl Harbor and inside the other destroyed ships. Like most of the other survivors, the pounding and tapping from the men who were trapped inside the ships and could not be rescued haunted him for a long time. It made Oscar feel so inadequate that he was unable to rescue more men. I'm sure that all of the rescue crew shared his anguish. Oscar had spent those three days following December 7th in a living hell. He told Mom and me that the most pitiful men were the ones who had suffered burns from the oil burning on the water. Many of these sailors died, and some of those who didn't claimed they wished that they had died. There were many joyous rescues, but they were darkly overshadowed by the loss of the men who could not be saved. There were a dreadful number of casualties, but the

The evidence of the attack that Bob found in his house.

48

Pieces from one of the Japanese submarines

rescuers were always proud that they had been able to help save some of their beloved shipmates. The Navy has always had a camaraderie that can't be beat.

One day Dad came rushing up the hill and loaded us into the car. "Come on," he said, "we have permission to go down to our house and gather up the things that we need."

They only gave us a short time, and whatever we took had to fit into the car. Everything else was left until a later time when the Navy went in, packed up our stuff and shipped it to us in the states. We got nearly everything, but we always wondered if there were a few boxes of our things sitting somewhere in a Navy warehouse. It was wartime, and if we had lost everything, it would not have been too surprising, nor too disappointing for that matter. We still had each other, and we knew that was what counted most.

As we drove down the hill and into our neighborhood, perhaps the most penetrating feeling was the total silence. No one was around, and the previously happy neighborhood stood there like a ghost town. As we drove toward our home on Jean Street, we could hardly believe the awful damage. We saw evidence of bombings and strafing and we also saw a downed Japanese plane that had crashed just a short distance from our home. There was a small resort hotel down by the water. It

One of the Japanese submarines that penetrated the harbor

had taken a direct hit from one of the Japanese planes as it crashed to the ground. The silence was eerie as we entered our house. We loaded the car with our necessary clothes, books, bookkeeping records, and some of Mom's most cherished photos. Dad needed all of his Navy clothing, and we took what food we could use up at the Vorfeld's house. The evidence of the attack was all around us, and we even found the remains of a bomb in our house. It was apparently a dud, because the house was still standing.

I was able to visit our house on Jean street several years later, while on a cruise with the Navy reserve, and it was, even then, still intact although I don't believe it was ever occupied again, and it has since been torn down. I picked up the remains of a few shells and debris, and shoved them in my pocket. I guess maybe I realized that we would never live there again, although it was hard to believe at the time. My whole life had been right there in Pearl City, and we had only lived in this one house, plus one other older house. We tied my bicycle on the back of the car, and I also grabbed my beloved fishing pole out of the garage where I had left it that awful Sunday morning, December 7th, 1941.

So we now began a life on the sugar plantation for about four months following the Pearl Harbor attack. I never returned to my Junior High School and the dreaded music lessons. I think they wanted to keep us closer to home, and so I was assigned to the August Ahrens School where I had spent my primary years. We had regular school hours and lessons, but there were some unusual activities compared to most schools. Workers came and cut slit trenches in the schoolyard. They were zigzagged lines that ran across the yard. We had air raid drills in which we were suppose to run and jump into a trench to help prevent us from being shot in case another attack came. They taught us which trench to jump into depending on which direction the enemy planes came from. Luckily we never had to try out this system, because there was no second attack at Pearl Harbor.

Those of us living in Hawaii tried to follow the lead of the citizens of the forty- eight states. We devoted much time and help to the war effort. The school children started purchasing war bond stamps. When we had the equivalent of $18.75 we could turn them in and get a war bond. We knew that in ten years our bonds would have grown to be worth $25.00. This was a good savings plan, but it also made us feel like we were helping to win the war. Because we had been there at Pearl Harbor, we felt so much a part of that war. We were all impressed when the song "Remember Pearl Harbor" became popular. The lines I remember are:

> *Let's remember Pearl Harbor*
> *As we go to meet the foe*
> *Let's remember Pearl Harbor*
> *As we did the Alamo*

The schools tried to help contribute to the war effort. We all helped the teachers plant a Victory Garden to grow vegetables, in case the food supply from the states was cut off. We tilled the soil, planted, watered and weeded. Our garden grew fairly well, too.

One day I got an unusual assignment. My teacher gave me money to go to the store in Waipahu and purchase some ladies' Kotex. The plan was to soak the sanitary napkins in Clorox to use to protect our breathing from poison gas—just in case. We never had to give this home made gas mask a try. I was relieved, as it always seemed that the Clorox might be more asphyxiating than the poison gas. I never knew if that was a valid idea.

Dad continued work at the base, but he could return to the sugar plantation and stay with us most nights. Because he had a fine mechanical mind with experience as a machinist, he was a very valuable person to have around. I always thought he was a hero, but he still felt bad that he couldn't do more. I was able to spend a great deal of time with Jack Vorfeld and his kids at the processing plant. We would go down to his office, and he would explain the wonders of processing sugar.

Saturdays were usually spent at the Waipahu Theatre. I became a member of the Buck Jones Club. Buck Jones was the hero of the film serial that ran weekly. The theatre would show the serial and newsreels of the war in Europe, and also a few coming attractions just before the feature film. The serial was a great attraction, as they always left poor Buck in a desperate life or death situation, so of course we wanted to return the next week to make sure he survived. Was there really ever any doubt that old Buck would survive?

One day at school the teacher said, "Hey Bobby, would you like to learn some First Aid?"

I had no idea what that was, but I was never one to argue, so I said, "okay." Sure enough that was worked into our daily lessons and we learned extremely basic first aid, such things as how to apply pressure to a wound and how to make a sling for a broken or damaged arm.

It was unsettling having to rub elbows on a daily basis with so many Japanese people. I knew a large number of them, but it was easy to wonder if the strangers were on the enemy's side. We would see them on weekends donning their kimonos and walking up the hill to their bathhouse. They heated the water with a wood fire, and they would get it good and hot and then go on inside. We were a little nervous to be so outnumbered by them, but none of them ever turned against us. The Japanese were caught in a terrible mess with their homeland of Japan attacking their adopted land. They were really in quite a fix. They tried their best to prove their loyalty, and kept their jobs at the plantation. As far as I know things calmed down and life went on as before, except for having extra people like us bunking at the plantation for four months.

MATSON NAVIGATION COMPANY   THE OCEANIC STEAMSHIP COMPANY

ALL PASSENGERS WERE GIVEN BAGGAGE DECLARATION FORMS, ADDRESS CARDS AND ETC. THIS MORNING, IT IS VERY IMPORTANT THAT YOU FILE THESE FORMS AT THE PURSER'S OFFICE TODAY.

LEAVE THIS PRESS REPORT SHEET IN YOUR STATEROOM. DO NOT TAKE IT ON DECK OR THROW IT, OR ANY OTHER PAPERS, OR REFUSE, OVER THE SIDE OF THE SHIP INTO THE WATER AT ANYTIME.

UNITED PRESS REPORTS ON THE WAR TODAY - - - - TUESDAY

JAPANESE PLANES BOMB INDIA CITIES

JAPAN CARRIED THE WAR TO INDIA today with attacks by sea-borne airplanes on two east coast cities. A strong enemy naval force, including aircraft carriers, was reported by the All-India radio to have attacked Allied shipping in the Bay of Bengal and sent small air squadrons to bomb the harbor at Vizagapatam and Cocanada. The Japanese squadron apparently had moved northward about 500 miles along the Indian coast after 75 of its airplanes attacked Colombo Harbor on the Island of Ceylon, where the British shot down 27 and downed or damaged probably 30 others. Enemy thrusts at India were timed with Axis propaganda broadcasts designed to disrupt British negotiations to bring an independent India into the war on the side of the United Nations. The Allied forces, however, also were striking hard at the enemy checking new Japanese attacks in the Philippines and knocking out more than 200 enemy airplanes over the week-end. The enemy attempts to break through American lines on Bataan at any cost resulted in a new thrust on land along the shores of Manila Bay and another over-water attack across the Bay, today's communique disclosed. Both were broken up with severe losses, including one dive bomber shot down after heavy fighting that checked the enemy offensive. No Japanese gains have been made since a slight advance Saturday. The Japanese also were renewing their twin drives in central Burma and Chungking reported some enemy forces had reached a point about 50 miles north of Prome where the British were trying to establish a new line in defense of the Burma oil fields. But in the air the Axis was suffering heavy losses on fronts scattered almost around the world and the British press estimated that the enemy had suffered a loss of 200 planes per week or about 2,600 aircraft since January 1, including more than 200 over the week-end.

AMERICAN FLYING FORTRESSES operating from India under Major Gen. Lewis H. Breton and with reinforced British fighter planes, were fighting to seize the initiative in the air and giving new strength to the combination of United States heavy bombers and crack British pursuit ships.

DISPATCHES FROM THE FIGHTING FRONTS INCLUDING:

BURMA -- Japanese land forces pushed north from Prome and Toungoo as American heavy bombers hammer the port of Rangoon, starting big fires.

CEYLON -- Natives search for Japanese pilots after Sunday's air battle in which 57 of 75 enemy planes, attacking from aircraft carriers, are downed or damaged in the worst defeat of the air war.

AUSTRALIA -- Thirty-five to 40 Japanese planes believed destroyed or damaged on the front north of Australia since Saturday. New enemy raids on Darwin and Port Moresby ineffective.

Shipboard newspaper that we received each day

The Journey Home

Sometime in early March 1942, a Navy officer showed up at the front door of the plantation house. "Is Florence Weber here?" he asked. Mom went apprehensively to the door. "Are you Mrs. Weber?

She answered with a hesitant, "Yes."

"I am here to inform you that you and your son will soon be evacuated to the United States."

"Where will we go?" she asked.

"Where is your home?" he inquired.

"My home is here in Pearl City," she said. "I have no other home."

"Do you have relatives stateside?" asked the officer.

"Yes," she replied. "My Father lives in Portland, Oregon."

"Then that's where you will go. We will call you 12 hours before the ship sails. We won't be able to give you any more notice than that for security reasons. Be ready with only one suitcase per person. Each person must be able to carry his own suitcase. It is suggested that you pack carefully so that you will have only the things that you really need."

So at last the phone call came. "Be at the dock at 0-six hundred," was the brief message. "Please bring only one suitcase per person.

The ship that brought us safely stateside

Make sure it is small enough for each person to carry his own. Do not bring anything else. This is all that will be allowed on board. This is a military operation, not a pleasure cruise. Conduct yourself accordingly."

We got up early and Dad came to drive us down to the dock. He was in a very subdued mood and Mom's mood matched his perfectly. As we arrived at the dock, we saw a large gathering of families starting to form. Dad hugged Mom, and then he hugged me. He turned back to Mom and said, "Here, take this flashlight. It's the only thing I have that I think you might be able to use." He turned to me and gave me my final orders, "Be a good kid, in fact, be a man and take care of your Mom. I'll keep praying for a terrible storm as you cross the ocean."

My mother was shocked, and asked, "Why in the world would you say a thing like that?"

"Hey, Dah, Da," his pet name for her, "take it easy. If it's stormy, the submarines won't be able to get their periscopes up and find you. The Captain's main job is to more or less hide you from the Japanese ships. A good storm would help him lots."

So then it was time to climb aboard the ship and start our journey.

We bid Dad another tearful farewell, and up the gangplank we trudged. It turned out that we had been on this ship once before, when we had traveled to the states to visit my grandparents. I believe the ship was the *Lurline*. If not, it was her sister ship in the Matson line, perhaps the *Matsonia*. It was a luxury liner that had been converted to a troop ship. It had been stateside for four months while being retrofitted as a military ship instead of being a luxury liner as it had been the last time we rode her to San Francisco. I was eager to look around, but first we had to sign in and receive our sleeping assignments from the Officer of the Day. At the same time we were given meal assignments and life jackets. They also had some sailors take us and show us where our lifeboat stations were located.

The entire ship was full of dependents and a few civilians, along with the official crew. Other than the crew, we were all considered non-essential to the war effort, so the decision was made to ship us to the states. We still had no way of knowing if the Japanese would return to Hawaii. It seemed rather unlikely after four months, but no one knew what the Japanese plans were. The luxury liner was barely recognizable from her former glory. She had been stripped of all unnecessary decorations, and they were replaced with only the essentials required to carry as many troops as possible.

We went down to our room assignments, which were down below the water line. Mom was a little disturbed that she could not bunk with me. They had chosen to have six boys about my age in a cabin together. She was next-door with five other women. Our room had three sets of bunk beds. All of us wanted the top bunks, so the bigger the boy, the better the chance that he got what he wanted. It seemed important at the time, but now I can't remember if I got a top bunk or not. One of the crew came by with clean sheets and the mothers each helped her own child get settled in his room and made their beds for them. As soon as things were in fair order, we heard a call over the loud speaker, "All hands and all guests report to the main dining room to get further instructions." This became the way we started out each morning. We reported to the dining room, and the Officer of the Day came into the room, and gave us the list of do's and don'ts.

These instructions were also printed on the daily ship's newspaper that was printed on board to keep us abreast of the happenings in the war and in the world. The newspaper was called the *Matson Line Wireless*. They were printed without dates, in case one fell into the water, so it wouldn't indicate to an enemy when we had sailed by. From the *Matson Line Wireless* we learned how the war was progressing. We read of war activity in far away places like India, Bataan, Burma, The Philippine Islands, New Guinea, Norway and London. Everyone was quite stricken on the day that we read that Bataan had fallen to the Japanese. Other than our daily instructions and the reports of war around the world, the newspaper would occasionally let us know what was happening in the world of sports. We learned that Babe Ruth was suffering from a bout with pneumonia, and we learned what Fala, President Roosevelt's Scottie dog, was up to.

Our daily orders included such items as these:

Wear your life jacket at all times!

Do not ever open the portholes or windows!

Complete blackout will be observed
from sunset to sunrise each day.

No smoking will be permitted on deck during blackout!

All passengers are forbidden to go on the boat deck, and are not permitted to go near the guns at the bow and the stern.

DO NOT THROW ANYTHING
OVERBOARD AT ANY TIME!

Everyone must be in his respective quarters by 10:00 p.m.

All unnecessary noise must cease at this hour.

And so it was time for the retrofitted troop ship to cast off and start our dangerous journey to the states. The weather was, as usual, warm and sunny, typical Hawaiian weather. We stood on deck and watched the Aloha Tower fade into the distance. We then set about the business of making new friends and searching out old friends who also had been sent to the states. It wasn't long before we got some unexpected entertainment as we watched a school of flying fish cavorting in the water and zooming through the air slightly above the waves. An impressive looking ship pulled up beside us, and it turned out to be our destroyer escort. It was loaded with depth charges in case of a run in with an enemy submarine. Our ship had guns, but no weapons to fight a deep-sea enemy. Our retrofitted luxury ship was a great deal larger and was able to cut through the water faster than the destroyer. Around noon of the second day, we started pulling ahead of the other ship. By the third day the destroyer was out of our sight. Luckily we never needed those depth charges. As we headed east, the Captain turned the ship in a zigzag course about every mile or so. Radar was a new item in the 1940s, so our ship was not blessed with it. Luckily the subs didn't have radar either. So the zigzag path was helpful from a safety standpoint.

For a ship overloaded with children, it was surprising how well behaved everyone was. There were several reasons for this. Our Dads had insisted on good behavior as we said goodbye in Hawaii. We also understood the seriousness of our situation. The Captain and crew kept emphasizing the importance of good behavior, and, frankly, at least half of the kids were too seasick to act up.

The sailors on board ship had many duties. Along with their regular tasks of running the ship, they served our meals, washed our laundry, and had the disgusting job of cleaning up after all the land-lubbers who didn't have their sea-legs and got sick and vomited repeatedly. I was lucky, as I never did get sick. I think my poor mother had some seasickness, but I was just a dumb kid wandering around enjoying the new experience, and trusting that the Navy would keep us safe.

Our stateroom was 2 decks below the water line. The smell from so many sick people was overwhelming. Mom took me topside as much as she could, and the fresh air was wonderful.

Because of the Captain's strict rule that the ship wouldn't stop for anyone who fell overboard, Mom chose to hold my hand whenever we were on deck. For a 12-year-old boy this was a tremendous humiliation, but of course I complied, because I knew it was just the way things were.

And so we continued our ocean journey to the U.S. mainland. We had plenty of provisions that had been brought to Hawaii from San Francisco on this same ship. The Navy didn't want to deplete food supplies in Hawaii, so they brought plenty for our journey to the mainland.

On about the sixth day, in the morning, a large blimp appeared and hovered over us. It was sent to help guide us to San Francisco. The first land we saw was the Farallon Islands. This meant we were very close to our destination. Before too long, the fog started to lift and there was the Golden Gate Bridge, a welcome sight indeed. Many passengers started cheering and crying.

Mom said, "Oh, Bobby, I remember the day you were born. We were on that small boat out in these waters drifting out to sea. Here we are again, going the opposite way."

And so I had come full circle. I began my life in San Francisco, born after a frightening boat ride. Now I was to begin the rest of my life, once again, in San Francisco, after an even more harrowing journey from Hawaii after the attack at Pearl Harbor. But we were safe, and Dad eventually returned safely to the states as a Chief Petty Officer. After the war he took us all to Shaniko, Oregon to see where his adventures had all begun.

Our family never again faced such a frightening situation. When I grew up I eventually joined the Navy during the Korean War. I was stationed the entire time on various bases all located in the States, from

California to Florida. I never again was in a place where I had to face the enemy. Pearl Harbor on December 7, 1941 was an experience that helped instill in me a lifetime of patriotism and so, of course, I shall always "Remember Pearl Harbor!"

Bob visiting Shaniko

Bob and Trinette Weber in 1998

*My thanks to those who helped me with this book.
Our children, Don, Marlis, and Lorraine,
and to Otto Papasadero, Connie Buckey, Mary Drabkin
and Tarky Hart for their help and advice.*

*And ever so much thanks to Myrna Oakley
who edited the book for me with much care and patience.*

To ORDER ADDITIONAL COPIES
send check or money order
for $14.95 + $2.50 shipping/handling to:
Trinette's
P. O. Box 69312
Portland, OR 97239

For questions or comments:
bobtrinette@aol.com